all of the thoughts i've thought about lately

Mattie Fry

all of the thoughts i've thought about lately
© 2022 Mattie Fry

All rights reserved.

No part of this publication may be
reproduced, stored in a retrieval system, or
transmitted, in any form or by any means,
electronic, mechanical, photocopying,
recording or otherwise, without the prior
written permission of the presenters.

Mattie Fry asserts the moral right to be
identified as author of this work.

Presentation by *BookLeaf Publishing*

Web: www.bookleafpub.com

E-mail: info@bookleafpub.com

ISBN: 9789357210515

First edition 2022

DEDICATION

Dedicated to Jason Welch, whom I've cried to, laughed with, and learned from. You are a human like no other, and I don't have enough words to explain the amount of goodness you have brought to this earth. Into my life. May you be forever proud of who you and what you do.

ACKNOWLEDGEMENT

Forever grateful for my two sisters, Katie and Allie, who push me towards my passions everyday. You have inspired me throughout my life and held me up in my lowest times. I love you squids.

PREFACE

I wrote this book as a challenge, to prove to myself I was capable of feeling again. Throughout the course of these poems, I prioritized my inner self, listening, focusing, and reflecting. I hope this book helps you to do the same.

out of reach

it was just a ghost of you,
I'll be honest.
a fading image of your gentle smile.
it hurt.
as you faded out,
and i faded back into reality,
without you.
I cried my tears,
said I was tired,
closed my eyes
and tried to find you
one
more
time.

prayers

im reaching for your memory,
grasping for your opinion,
your guidance.
it's why I say your name,
in place of God,
because at least I knew you were real.

body - mind

3

I'd kiss every inch of my body.
I'd hug and accept all of it.
However it's getting quite harder to ignore
this stupid mind of mine.

seasonal

hot cocoa and winter and falling star wishes.
you took all I had when you gave me those
kisses.

oranges and summer and your quick dismisses
you've caused all this pain and still you're the
one my heart misses.

day by day

for a few days I feel joy and calmness like I've
always dreamt of.
then, like food poisoning it comes out of
nowhere
and anything that made me smile yesterday is
twisted into something cruel,
my eyes well at the memory of yesterday,
why did the world let me be happy one day
and empty all the next

solo

How can you all feel so unfamiliar?
I am sitting in this chair suffocating under this
face,
falsifying who I am before your eyes.
Too outnumbered to speak.
Too fucking high to want to.
I sit as though I am alone.

Perhaps it's because I've spent my life being the
middleman,
playing fix it and mediator.
Lowering the volume of arguments, smiling
through this rage,
and observing every insignificant interaction,
weaving together intricate stories of who I'm
pretending to be.

I miss feeling comfort, adrenaline, happiness.
My presence has been deemed only worthy as a
distraction.
And they wonder why I wither into nothing,
as though it wasn't their hands around my bony
neck,
like it wasn't their fingers jabbing into over
stretched skin,

like the words that spilled from their mouths
didn't steal all the breath in these lungs.

7

too much time

8

I hate writing poetry that rhymes.
It's way to hard and takes too much time.
But in the off chance that I do,
I certainly won't write of you.

boss woman

it wasn't until i met you that i truly understood
what conversation really was,
to stand firmly in my emotions.
expressing my difference in opinion didn't need
to cause me anxiety,
instead you showed me a casual conversation.
you exemplified understanding and
comprehension.
you gathered everything i told you and gave the
best response you had.
every time.
for this I will always hold you dear,
since you were never too good to open your
ears.

none

I gave you all of my everything.
Attention.
Attraction.
Time.

Now how do I move on with nothing.
No apology.
No explanation.
No history.
As though you have erased me.

Now I give none of me to anyone.
With the hope that someone,
is out there,
with something.

dinner time

while i wash my vegetables i think about cold
water,
i dry them and wonder why i never got in
farther.
as i slice each one my hands remember the feel
of precision,
the onion fumes now blurring my vision.
a certain steadiness within this kitchen,
i dance back and fourth while my body finds
rythmn.
the scent of paprika and oregano floating
through the air,
and i whisk and stir without a single care.
it's art and it's peace, a comfort in creating,
a meal where there are people patiently
awaiting.

in silence

it is within milliseconds of or eyes meeting
that my body is consumed by an overwhelming
craving for you.
the my adrenaline levels are climbing so high
that if your fingers were to graze me even the
slightest,
i think my heart my beat out of my chest.
it's thundering cant you hear it?

if i stand to close to someone i fear they might
feel the ground around me quaking,
the strength that, at one time, ran through my
fingers has dissipated into nothing more than a
dull attempt at coordination.

you are my body high
the infinite possible interactions fill the forefront
of my mind
and i am unable to focus on anything more than
the sound of your voice and the color of your
eyes,
strategically planning my movement,
preying for the ecstasy of your touch.

lenses

to see the world through my eyes,
what a confusing world you would see.
strings uniting every human
and branches connecting every tree.
where energy flowed clearly,
everything pictured in its simplest form,
the inconvenience of cruelty,
with ease and peace I can mourn.

I cannot make you see the world I do,
though I very much would like to.
Instead I can try and see the world as you do,
and from there we'll go and find you.

what i've learned from listening:

1.) some feelings just need to be felt first
2.) speak when you know what you want to say
3.) open ears are worth much more than an open mouth
4.) holding their hands says more than you know
5.) communicate acceptance
6.) honesty saves everyone's time
7.) seeing both sides is educating not betraying
8.) after listening, its much easier to be heard

ecc

you all never fail to make me laugh,
really laugh,
where my eyes get real squinty and start to
water,
where my stomach starts to ache and it gets hard
to breathe.
and we laugh together with joy.
and we are all friends.

we'll have a story for anyone and everyone
who'd like to hear,
an obstacle that's being overcome,
or an answer you never knew you needed.
please join our conversation,
we would love to know your name.
who you are and where you're going.

order yourself a cup of coffee,
pull up a seat,
and may we laugh together through the morning.

slo

today i bought a candle that smells like you.
it smells like a dusty flannel, or the vague
remnants of your morning cologne.
but it smells clean and soft, like your bed sheets
on those nights.
it smells like comfort and safety,
in the arms of a man who was never my partner
but always my friend.
it smells the man that protected me and held me
as i fell apart.
this candle is a sixteen and a half ounce
reminder of the boy who feels like home.
when were miles away and i was lost and afraid,
i fell into you.
and now this candle smells like the question
mark
at the end of every single what if we were more?
but i don't think ill burn this candle because
sometimes its just easier to hold to a piece of
home,
even if i've moved out.

earthquaking

i think i was born with an earthquake inside me,
a constant energy rippling throughout my body,
my mind.
a seismic wave that drowns me.
an overwhelming consciousness that shoots
through my spine
my hands making me aware that my body might
not just be able to handle my mind.
so while my earth quakes i breathe, and find
stillness in the rumbling
and my ground settles back into silence.

T

you, my friend are not all sadness and loss,
you are beauty and strength, confidence and
radiance.
you are more than any man could ever give you.
i've seen you laugh and cry and heard you
scream and cheer,
it is within these many faces of you that i came
to value you as my closest friend.
no matter the hurt or the struggle, you continue
to give more than you have,
but sweetheart you cannot endure this pain with
nothing,
you must fill your cup before filling anyone
else's.

happy place

i have made a home in my head.
a place where the walls are painted in memories
and nostalgia,
the floors made up of every place i've ever been.
it is my biggest accomplishment, to need
nothing and no-one more than myself.
my mind is a place that accepts all thoughts and
opens conversations no-one would imagine.
my world is so much larger now, the people so
much more interesting.
my heart is overfilling with love to give now.
at night, all alone, my bed is still warm, even
when i'm the only one in it.

have a great summer

the summer is both my least and most favorite
season.
sunshine is warm but i somehow always end up
burned
the fruits are so sweet but the flies are soon to
follow
i love the slightly warmer rivers and pools,
where the chill only hits when your leaving.
but my eyes close more and more as the days go
on, as my blue eyes slowly burn.
the fresh a/c in the grocery stores
then the searing black leather seats in my car
cold and refreshing sweet iced tea
sticky sweat droplets sprinting down my back.
the summer can be warm and bright, but also
burning and depleting.
much like many of us.

caramel macchiato

21

a hot silver milk pitcher warming my cold shaky
hands,
the swirling inflation of liquid screams a song of
unique serenity.
then the bottom of soft paper cup coated in
caramel,
caramel that smells like summer apples and
smiling faces,
and vanilla swimming carefully through golden
sweetened swirls.
espresso that's smooth, without teeth to bite the
back of my throat as i swallow.
stirred together with love as the flavors meet on
another for the first time.
topped with fluffy whipped.
a delightful way to start the morning and fill
your heart with warmth.

to feel

i feel love
on those hot but overcast days where my eyes
can fully open,
the a/c in my car is blowing, it doesn't even
matter where i'm driving.
i feel love
in the rhythm of a song i hadn't appreciated this
much before,
my hands dance around with fluidity and
freedom, my heart beats right along.
i feel love
when my hands are grasping another's,
grounding me into this reality, where everyone's
worlds are intertwined.
i feel love
after months of numbness the air in my lungs
feels fresh again,
the sun feels warm and my smiles are real.
and i am finally alive.